A Time To Turn...
THE PASCHAL EXPERIENCE

Anita M. Constance, S.C.

PAULIST PRESS • New York/Mahwah

Cover and interior illustrations by Anne Haarer, S.C.

Cover design by James F. Brisson.

Interior design by Saija Autrand, Faces Type & Design.

Library of Congress Cataloging-in-Publication Data

Constance, Anita M., 1945–
    A time to turn : the Paschal experience / Anita M. Constance.
      p. cm.
    ISBN 0-8091-3613-9 (alk. paper)
    1. Paschal mystery—Prayer-books and devotions—English.
  2. Catholic Church—Prayer-books and devotions—English.
  3. Devotional calendars. I. Title.
    BX2170.P328C66 1995
    242'.3—dc20   95-35390
                                                                    CIP

Published by Paulist Press
997 Macarthur Boulevard
Mahwah, N.J. 07430

Printed and bound in the United States of America

CONTENTS

DEDICATION

to Maria Regis Kentz, S.C.

soul-friend

ACKNOWLEDGMENTS

Often we are gifted with persons who come into our lives quite unexpectedly. Some stay to bless us with friendship, others move on after only a short time . . . and others return. Still connections are made and gifts are exchanged.

Special thanks must be given to **Msgr. Joseph J. Gallo** (Diocese of Paterson, New Jersey) who contributed the series of prose reflections found in ***A Time To Turn.*** His free and intuitive style of presentation has added a focus to the Sundays of Lent and Easter which draws the reader to a central theme and encourages one to think more deeply about God's word and grace during this season of reflection, conversion and praise.

I feel a turning point...
    A point of no return?
    No.
    I've been this way before,
    but not quite.

How many times do we pass through
    the same place
    only to find it new
    again and again?

I walk ... climb ...
    a spiral staircase
    through a mansion
    or a castle
    or a seven-story mountain.

I feel a turning point...
    A point of no return?
    No.
    I've been this way before,
    but not quite.

INTRODUCTION

During Lent, the church invites us to make the journey inward. Our destination is God. Our path is transformation. Conversion depends upon our commitment and God's grace. Yet, it is the grace of God that keeps us in the direction of our desire and goal. We are drawn toward the light, aware of our shadow but never overcome by its darkness. Sin is not so much a turning away from the light as it is a refusal to advance.... We stand still, fixed in the moment by weakness of will.

Yet God is always aware of us, always aware of what is yet unhealed. In Jesus Christ, God embraces that human limitation. Through him, God reaches out, untiringly, and says, "Yes.... Come to me." And so, we turn with confidence knowing God has already turned to us. We leave self-protection behind and again choose life. God's invitation enables us to release life's securities in order to obtain life anew. Such openness to God is an act of faith which acknowledges our dependence, yet expresses a commitment to God's faithful love.... Necessity pushes us where virtue has not yet led.

A Time To Turn is an opportunity to set our faces toward the Light. To become aware of our shadow, confident that God still draws us near. To renew our commitment to God's faithful love. This is a journey we will make again and again. We were not born in pieces, but it requires a lifetime to discover our wholeness— the fullness of God's original intention.

A Time To Turn penetrates the very heart of the Paschal Mystery, planting us in the daily experience of death and resurrection. This is a book for the people of God because we are never alone in our turning. Our brothers and sisters not only join us on the journey, they are essential to it. Conversion catches us up in one another. We cannot escape this reality. Its truth meets us at every turn. Always and forever, God throws us back into the arms of brother and sister and says, "Here I Am!"

ASH WEDNESDAY

Jesus said to his disciples: "Be on guard against performing religious acts for people to see.... In giving alms you are not to let your left hand know what your right hand is doing.... Whenever you pray, go to your room, close your door, and pray to your Father in private.... When you fast, see to it that you groom your hair and wash your face ... your Father who sees what is hidden will repay you" (Mt 6:1–6, 16–18).

We turn round, O God,
and round and round—
each year, each day ...
in search of our home
which is you.
You are a gracious host,
patient with our wanderings,
steadfast with blessings
at an open door.
Cast compassion before us,
as crumbs,
that we might find
our way to you.
Wash away the guilt
that burdens us with fear
and faltering steps.

Turn our eyes toward you.
Grant us a depth of vision
that sees into your heart
and celebrates
the sleight of hand.

May our prayers
abandon city streets
for the quiet corners
of truth—
and there,
in letting go,
may we be held fast
by Jesus
whose embrace graced
the cross
and hastened holiness
home. Amen.

The Turning:

What is lost to my eyes is found in God's vision.

I am invited to let go ... to let reality, with all its threatening unpredictability, bless my life.

....

....

....

THURSDAY

Then he [Jesus] said to them all, "If any want to become my followers, let them deny themselves and take up their cross daily and follow me. For those who want to save their life will lose it, and those who lose their life for my sake will save it. What does it profit them if they gain the whole world, but lose or forfeit themselves?" (Lk 9:23–25, NRSV).

God of fullness,
you blessed our lives
with height and depth,
choices and opportunities.
How gracious
your gift of freedom
birthed in our beginnings,
fleshed out on the path
between life and death.

Your call to life
is held in delicate balance
on the beams of a cross.
Your gift of hope
rests in the roots
of that tree
where we ponder
   the wisdom
of lost and found.

Followers
of a crucified Christ,
we are tempted
to drag our feet.

Suffering and rejection
are bitter pills
from the physician
of new life.
Profit is our protection,
yet forfeit is the price.

God of our longing,
free us from ourselves.
May your invitation
to mystery
encourage the risking.
Remind us
that to follow
is child-meekness,
to lose ... the threshold
of finding,
and to die ...
the dawn of new life. Amen.

The Turning:

Jesus invites me to enter the growth process by dying with him. I am called to wholeness by shocking paradox and costly terms.

Commitment does not come easily. "Yes" is never spoken without struggle.

....

....

3

*This, rather, is the fasting that I wish: releasing those bound un-
justly.... Setting free the oppressed.... Sharing your bread with
the hungry, sheltering the oppressed and the homeless.... Then
your light shall break forth like the dawn, and your wound shall
quickly be healed (Is 58:6–8).*

God of integrity,
we cannot mislead you
with fasts
or sacrifice worn
to clothe a deceitful heart.
You meet us
at the point of truth
and do not relent
in your demands
for sincerity of heart.

You call us
to put flesh
on the bones of justice—
To recognize companions
of hunger.
To fill hearts
empty of love.
To welcome wanderers
home, and
break the chains
of controlling wills.

Teach us to see,
to gather, to lift
and to free.
Let your light
break open shadows
cast by the selfishness
of broken promises.

Help us to wholeness.
Heal what separates us
from one another
that we might be held
by hope. Amen.

The Turning:

The gospel, not lived, is like a seed that never meets the ground.

As I hunger for the bread of contemplation ... Jesus invites me
to the banquet of compassion.

....

....

....

....

SATURDAY

Levi gave a great reception for Jesus in his house. . . . The Pharisees and the scribes . . . said to his disciples, "Why do you eat and drink with tax collectors and non-observers of the law?" Jesus said to them, "The healthy do not need a doctor; sick people do. I have not come to invite the self-righteous to a change of heart, but sinners" (Lk 5:29–32).

God of hospitality,
you walk with sinners
to companion
our conversion.
You place yourself
among the weak
and there invite
our strength.

While we pursue
our own affairs,
you pursue us
with unbounding hope
and relentless grace.

Your hand of welcome
opens wide
and blessings
tumble forth . . .

caught by us,
yet called by you
to let them
slip
through our fingers . . .
to become bread
and light and healing
for one another.

Continue to spread
your table before us,
O God.
With Jesus,
let us stand
at the door
and call one another
home.
May we find a place
in one another
that is love and life,
fullness and healing. Amen.

The Turning:

I know Jesus in the breaking of the bread when I am willing to share my life with another.

I am challenged to break away from "conditions" in order to know the "unconditional."

....

....

....

....

SUNDAY

The Big Lie

At the heart of all temptation is "The Big Lie." It is spoken by the serpent when he promises Adam and Eve that they will "become like gods" when they eat the forbidden fruit, and again by Satan when he shows Jesus all the kingdoms of the earth, and promises, "All these I will give you, if you will fall down and worship me" (Mt 4:9, NRSV).

Each of us, being created in the image of God, is endowed with the incomparable gift of freedom. Ultimately we come to realize the unlimited possibilities this gift opens to us. We can be easily tempted to "want it all," to become "like gods." The world, the flesh and the devil whisper "The Big Lie" in many deceptive ways. But we learn, often by bitter experience, that, if our search is limited to created and material things only, we are doomed to failure, frustration and emptiness.

The words of Jesus come thundering out of the desert: "One does not live by bread alone.... Worship the Lord your God, and serve only him" (Mt 4:4, 10, NRSV). During the season of Lent we seek to clarify our vision of faith, so that we will be able to recognize "The Big Lie." This time of prayer, fasting and service helps us to redefine our priorities. It is a unique season of grace, a period of special openness to the movements of the Spirit, enabling us to discern more clearly that our deepest hungers will only be satisfied when we perfect the art of loving God above all things and neighbor as self.

Let that be our "menu" for Lent.

GOSPELS: Cycle A—Mt 4:1–11
Cycle B—Mk 1:12–15
Cycle C—Lk 4:1–13

God of creation,
you formed us
in hope and goodness—
in your image and likeness.
But we struggle, Lord.
We struggle
to continue the molding
of our lives
to become worthy
of our inheritance ...
to become worthy of you.

Yet,
will we ever be?
Each day
we face the choice
of good or evil.
We try, Lord ...
still
we are clumsy
with this great gift—
the freedom
that you give us.

But
sin does not keep you
from love.
Sin does not keep you
from thoughts of salvation.
Should we despair
of you,
you would not despair
of us
for you gave us Jesus
to return us to you.

Bless our efforts
toward good
and forgive the times
we choose poorly.
May Jesus be
our bread of life,
his Spirit
the only power we seek,
your holy presence
the only value
worthy of worship and praise.
Amen.

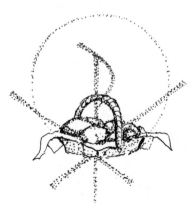

"Come, you that are blessed by my Father, inherit the kingdom prepared for you from the foundation of the world; for I was hungry and you gave me food, I was thirsty and you gave me something to drink, I was a stranger and you welcomed me, I was naked and you gave me clothing, I was sick and you took care of me, I was in prison and you visited me.... Truly I tell you, just as you did it to one of the least of these who are members of my family, you did it to me" (Mt 25:34–36, 40, NRSV).

Holy God,
you are the root
of our righteousness ...
our right-ness.
Out of your holiness,
you call us to wholeness.
You visit us
in one another
through integrity of heart.
From the center
of mystery
you reveal your presence
as flesh-in-action.
You draw the thread
of communion
from being to being
to being,
and weave a garment
meant to clothe
all of human life.

No display of devotion
can replace
the embrace of you.
We cannot dodge
dedication
with words that flower
the power of love....
Your knowing
sharpens us to focus.

Inexhaustible
fountain of truth,
let the waters
that stirred life
at Baptism
carry us along the ways
of faith,
usher us into the halls
of hope
and flood our hearts
with love. Amen.

The Turning:

I am overwhelmed by the hunger and poverty of the world around me. Where do I begin? I begin with what I have ... I begin with myself.

Grace for the long haul keeps me faithful in the face of limitation.

....

....

Give us today our daily bread, and forgive us the wrong we have done as we forgive those who wrong us (Mt 6:11–12).

God of love,
we praise your name
in Jesus—
your Word of Life!
He is the seed
planted in our hearts
from the beginning
of time.
He is your blessing
fallen from the heavens
like rain,
penetrating roots
grounded in you.

Jesus calls us
to lift hands
and heart to you,
who embrace
our needs
and cradle them
in daily bread.
He leads us to
forgiveness,
inviting us across
the bridge
of alienation
to heal wounds
that fester
far beyond skin-deep...
clearing the pathway
to peace
for one another.

You know our need
for you, O God,
before we know
that need.
Turn our minds
toward you.
Let us focus
our day
through the lens
of your wisdom,
that we may see
holiness
in our everyday
and know your will
like brailled images
present
to the touch. Amen.

The Turning:

When God looks for me at the feast of forgiveness, will God find me there?

Forgiveness moves me from destruction to blessing.

....

....

....

....

When the crowds were increasing, he began to say, "This generation is an evil generation; it asks for a sign, but no sign will be given to it except the sign of Jonah. For just as Jonah became a sign to the people of Nineveh, so the Son of Man will be to this generation." (Lk 11:29–30, NRSV).

God of forgiveness,
we often do
what we desire not,
and grovel
in dust of our own
making—
slow to raise
our eyes to you.
Instead,
you ask us
to celebrate
sackcloth and ashes.
You invite us
to look guilt
in the eye—
a hard, honest stare—
and proclaim the grace
of Resurrection,
for you are greater
than sin and
stronger than death.

Help us
to live the signs
of conversion
today—
to don
sacrifice for sackcloth,
to trade
action for ashes.
Let time cast
the sign of prophets
in hearts of flesh.

May we give way
to your touch
and follow the freedom
carved by Christ.
Let us use this
occasion of grace
to celebrate
inner strength . . .
through the saving
courage of Jesus. Amen.

The Turning:

Even when I fail, God does not abandon me. God leads me to new beginnings.

If Jesus died that I may have life, I must get on with the business of living.

....

....

....

....

Queen Esther prayed, "My Lord, our King, you alone are God. Help me, who am alone and have no help but you.... Manifest yourself in the time of our distress and give me courage" (Est C 12:16, 23).

Faithful God,
you alone
are our help,
and so

We pray...
Rock of Refuge,
and find peace
as we lean into the ledge
of your protection
carved for us.

We pray...
Rock of Comfort,
in whose warm, strong
shadow we rest
and are refreshed.

We pray...
Rock of Safety,
whose heights we climb
when the shores of life
are threatened
by troubled waters.

We pray...
Rock of Courage,
whose steadfast presence
enables us
to hold on
through the night.

We pray...
Rock of Wisdom,
who allows us
to stand on high
and sight our world
with clearer vision.

We pray...
Rock of Solitude,
as we thirst
for aloneness
and drink
of your stillness.

We pray...

Amen.

The Turning:

Prayer carries me from doubt to faith, from hesitancy to confidence.

The presence of God is not dependent upon my knowing or not knowing. My crying out, my prayer, asserts God's presence as well as my need.

....

....

....

So when you are offering your gift at the altar, if you remember that your brother or sister has something against you, leave your gift there before the altar and go; first be reconciled to your brother or sister, and then come and offer your gift (Mt 5:23–24, NRSV).

God of justice,
the road
to reconciliation
is a path
hard to tread
at times.
Vengeance and pride
pull us, push us,
prevent us even
from walking
side by side
on the way
to healing.

Time is precious.
Let us not
squander it
searching
for the eye and tooth
of self-righteousness.

Instead, let us
hold one another
as gifts ...
offering forgiveness
at your altar.
Let our dignity
not come
from exacting
a price, but
from a sacrifice
of love—
offered for us
by your Son,
Jesus.

Let this
be the prayer
that rises from
the temple
of our hearts ...
to give you
glory. Amen.

The Turning:

Do I really know what is in another's heart?

Forgiveness helps me to the other side of hurt, remorse and guilt. Once across, I have a view from the other's side.

....
....
....
....

You have heard that it was said, "You shall love your neighbor and hate your enemy." But I say to you, "Love your enemies, and pray for those who persecute you, so that you may be children of your Father in heaven.... For if you love those who love you, what reward do you have?... And if you greet only your brothers and sisters, what more are you doing than others?" (Mt 5:43–47, NRSV).

God of promise,
it is you who
first
held out a
covenant-hand
to us...
leading us
from the desert
of despair
to the fertile ground
of hope—
we, a people
sacred to you.

In Jesus,
you reveal
the holy fibers
of our bonding—
thread upon thread
of inescapable
love.

The cost
of this communion
is not
flesh for flesh,
but life...
for life.

Help us
to love those
who love us not.
Keep us from
storming
our way into
their lives
with ridicule
and discontent.
Remind us
to examine the health
of our own hearts,
and the integrity
of those intentions.

Let us look
first
to ourselves
for covenant response.
Then, may our seeing
inward
lead us out
to others—
weaving
thread upon thread
of inescapable
love. Amen.

The Turning:

The kingdom of God is not a system of weights and measures. Winning and losing are tensions, never healers.

Jesus did not balance the scales of justice with a pound of flesh. He balanced them with forgiveness.

SUNDAY

Surprises on the Mountaintop

It started out to be a routine climb to the mountaintop for some quiet prayer time with Jesus; it turned out to be a wondrous, unforgettable experience: his transfiguration. The apostles weren't sure if it was a vision, a dream, or an illusion, but they did know that it was good to be there. They wanted the moment to last forever. Even after they returned to the valley of reality, the dazzling image of the transfigured Lord would stay with them, especially during the dark days of suffering and near despair.

There are surprises waiting for all of us on the mountaintop of faith. We are amazed again and again at the incredible power and resiliency of the human spirit when it is fired by trust in God. We all experience those high moments when we seem to be transformed. We achieve the impossible. We discover within ourselves resources we never dreamed were there. We are capable of heroic love and generosity. Yes, we too want those moments to last forever. Yet, when we must go back down to the valley of reality, the memory of those surprising victories stays with us and sustains us.

Our faith in Jesus leads us to look forward to the ultimate transformation that is resurrection. So we journey through this Lent, and all our Lents, in the joyful hope that one day we shall experience the final and unending surprise that awaits us. When we complete our journey through the valley of death to arrive at the mountaintop, the risen Lord will welcome us to share his victory forever.

GOSPELS: Cycle A—Mt 17: 1–9
                    Cycle B—Mk 9:2–10
                    Cycle C—Lk 9:28b–36

God of truth,
a blessing you promised
and a blessing
you give.
Through deserts
and up mountains
we follow Jesus
and there find you ...
and ourselves
as we were meant to be.

We long
to hold on to
that vision, O God.
We try
to set up tents
and stay
as long as we can,
because it is there
that we know
we are truly home.

But
faith calls us,
for it was
in faith
that Jesus lived life
and accepted death.
His faith in you
was born of love.
His love
was born of freedom.

In Jesus,
the bright cloud
of your grace
is forever upon us.
May we be willing
to leave
the mountaintop
experiences
of life
and walk the plains
of every day. Amen.

Jesus said to his disciples: "Be compassionate, as your Father is compassionate.... For the measure you measure with will be measured back to you" (Lk 6:36–38).

God of unconditional love,
of freedom
beyond-all-measure ...
how do we fathom
within
our own hearts
a depth of self-giving
so much more
than our experience?
How do we enter
your boundless
generosity,
for we measure not
beyond-all-measure?

Help us, O God ...
Help us
to exchange the weight
of judgment
for the freedom
of forgiveness.

To clothe
our brothers and sisters
with the garment
of compassion.
To let mercy
make a home
in our hearts,
and truth
the door through which
we pass ...
And there
so enter upon
the way of Jesus
who is life
beyond-all-measure. Amen

The Turning:

When God throws the doors to the kingdom wide open, will I question such generosity ... or will I welcome the guests?

Nothing is lost. It is just the cost of loving.

....
....
....
....
....
....

The greatest among you will be your servant. All who exalt themselves will be humbled, and all who humble themselves will be exalted (Mt 23:11–12, NRSV).

God of truth,
you seek us
at the heart
of what matters.
Your gaze
goes further
than the human eye.
Words are empty
unless they frame
our faith
with flesh.

In Jesus,
desire and will
meet . . .
truth and justice
embrace.
Through Jesus,
the weight
of empty practices
was lifted . . .
freedom
filled choices
and fired sacrifice.

With Jesus,
the bonds of pride
were broken—
and the seat of humility
honored.

In the spirit
of Jesus, then,
may our vision
meet your gaze,
our words
be made flesh,
our desire
fire our will
and freedom
fill all that we
embrace—
fulfilling
your covenant
of servant-love. Amen.

The Turning:

I have been invited into a kingdom where humility reigns and forgiveness is a way of life. It is the wealth of this kingdom that I am called to distribute.

I do not "gain" heaven. I grow accustomed to it here on earth—by helping to create it.

....

....

....

"Promise me that these sons of mine will sit, one at your right hand and the other at your left, in your kingdom." In reply Jesus said, "You do not know what you are asking. Can you drink of the cup I am to drink of?" (Mt 20:21–22).

O God,
your kingdom
is not one of
conflict and power,
but one of
kinship.
You desire
relationship
not rivalry
and so empower
greatness
with humility,
and meekness
with strength.
Places of honor
are wounds in
your right hand
and left.

With our brother,
Jesus,
you bid us
gather 'round
and share a cup
of blood and tears . . .
to drink death
before the promised
dawn.

How foolish we are
to think that pushing
our way to you
avoids the pull
of one another.
Forgive . . . forgive us
who look for answers
in a balance
of heaven and earth
but leave no room
for the ballast
of your wisdom.
Forgive us the egos
that edge you out
of our holiness. Amen.

The Turning:

God does not take away conflict or pain. God offers me healing within and blessing throughout.

To make the journey inward, some former concepts are shattered like glass. These cut into the heart of discipleship and carve new hope.

Once there was a rich man who ... feasted splendidly every day.
At his gate lay a beggar named Lazarus. ... Lazarus longed to
eat the scraps that fell from the rich man's table (Lk 16:19–21).

God of goodness,
how many times
have we passed
through the door
of our homes
and missed
the hungers of you?
We find ourselves
laden with bread,
yet many
still cry for
mere crumbs.

What is wrong
with our vision?
Why does it
tunnel
down our paths
and capture
only the poor
of our choosing?
Why are we
so narrow
in defining needs?

Jesus sensed
what could not
be seen
and
noticed needs
as in rhythm
with his every breath.

Teach us
through him
to be attentive
to our actions,
worthy
of our words,
generous
with our giving—
so that another's
thirst
may reach our own
throats
and be satisfied
by the cooling
waters of our
compassion. Amen.

The Turning:

If I allow myself to get so cushioned by life that my vision never
sees beyond the door of my home, I will suffer from a poverty of
heart—empty of compassion and love. And, in the end, I may lose
my humanity.

I must not separate God from my experience.

....

....

....

Finally he sent his son to them, thinking, "They will respect my son." When they saw the son, the tenants said to one another, "Here is the one who will inherit everything. Let us kill him and then we shall have his inheritance!" (Mt 21:37–38).

O God,
the giver
of all good gifts
why do we
reject
your generous share
of water and Spirit?

You offer
fullness of life
in a son
and brother,
but greed
turns
our hearts away
and jealousy
deadens
our hearing.

Yet
what we reject,
you accept!

Your grace
brightens the shadows
cast
by our turning,
and so confounds
the darkness
with light—
our hope in Jesus Christ.

Break open our deafness,
O God.
Let your Word,
Jesus,
penetrate our hearts
like rain,
and soften them
to willing flesh.

Let that Word
mend
what is broken
and open
the path
of our return. Amen.

The Turning:

Jesus performed miracles that inspired some to faith and others to fear.

The kingdom of God: to offer forgiveness when I do not understand ... to speak peace when power seems the quicker solution ... to encourage change when no change is acceptable ... to resist the comfort of the crowd ... to speak life in the face of death.

....

....

"I will break away and return to my father...." While he was still a long way off, his father caught sight of him and was deeply moved. He ran out to meet him, threw his arms around his neck, and kissed him (Lk 15:18, 20).

O God,
you spread arms
of mercy
toward us.
You embrace us
in forgiveness
and love.
You accept us
as we are
and allow
our wanderings ...
as freedom's gift.

Yet ...
we are never
out of sight
for you.
Never
so far away
that your heart
does not beat
in rhythm with ours.

Continue
to keep us
close to you,
despite the distance
we lay between.

Wait
to greet us
at the moment
of our return
for
we are often
timid, and walk
with steps
caught in guilt
along the way.

Help us
to realize
you bond us
with love ...
only love.
Let that knowing
encourage
our turning. Amen.

The Turning:

Not forgive and forget, but forgive and accept. God gave me the gift of memory, but also the freedom to move on.

To acknowledge my sin is to celebrate God's mercy.... God does not require a pure heart before embracing me.

....
....
....

SUNDAY

Going to the Well

Our journey through Lent can be described as "going to the well." We are dusty and thirsty from our travels; we need to be refreshed and cleansed. We make our way to the well of the Spirit which we find in prayer and sacrament. Jesus is waiting there for us. In his presence, we become more aware of our thirst and hungers. He invites us again to drink deeply of the waters of faith, promising that this living water will become a fountain within us, leaping up to provide forgiveness, healing, wholeness, and a foretaste of eternal life.

In the waters of baptism, we were reborn to newness of life and sealed with the Spirit of God. Authentic conversion should produce the fruits of holiness and justice. For most of us, it is a long, slow process with many setbacks and failures. But the Lord is patient and long-suffering. He gives us the opportunity to "come to the well" often.

St. Paul writes: "Let us profess the truth in love and grow to the full maturity of Christ" (Eph 4:15). Lent may call us to the practice of self-denial, yet it is more a time for growing up than for giving up. It is also a time for living faith and sharing faith. Like the Samaritan woman we must become evangelists. The quality of our daily lives must announce the good news to others, and invite them to "come to the well" to discover in Jesus the healing and peace that we enjoy.

GOSPELS: Cycle A—Jn 4:5–42
Cycle B—Jn 2:13–25
Cycle C—Lk 13:1–9

God of forgiveness,
you see us as
we truly are—
whole yet broken,
strong though weak,
certain yet still afraid.

Sometimes our hearts
are dry as stone
or hollow
as an empty well.
You come
into our lives
to strike the stone
and call forth
living waters.
You fill the well
of our lives
to overflowing.

In Jesus,
you invite us
to find power
in weakness
and freedom
in vulnerability.

In Jesus,
you drive away falsehood,
call for honesty of heart
and integrity of spirit.
You challenge us
to use our gifts rightly
and to believe
in the grace of your Word.

Give us wisdom
that responds to
conversion
and humility
that recognizes
the temple that
is human flesh—
the holy place
wherein you dwell.

May we die
to the images of self
that we carve,
and be held
by the hope
of that holiness. Amen.

"No prophet gains acceptance in his native place. . . . Recall, too, the many lepers in Israel in the time of Elisha the prophet; yet not one was cured except Naaman the Syrian." At these words the whole audience in the synagogue was filled with indignation (Lk 4:24, 27–28).

O God,
who call us
to be your own,
election
is not exclusive—
and so
we find
strangers
in the fold
of your embrace.

Titles do not
seal your choice.
Instead,
your image
printed
on the heart
of daily living
is cause enough.
Election
embraces
faith-in-action.

Who are we
to reject
your definition
of family then,
and fling aside
brothers and sisters
. . . jealous
of your generosity?

Open our minds.
Free us from
the fear that
space for others
will replace us.
Open our eyes.
Lift the veil
that values
distinction
without integrity.
May the character
of the kingdom
be cause enough. Amen.

The Turning:

Lord, keep me from the illusion of being "singular," for then I build a wall between myself and others.

Do I doubt the truths of God, or do I fear what they will mean to my life?

....

....

....

Peter came and said to him, "Lord, if another member of the church sins against me, how often should I forgive? As many as seven times?" Jesus said to him, "Not seven times, but, I tell you, seventy-seven times" (Mt 18:21-22, NRSV).

O God,
you created us
with the soul
of forgiveness.
In Jesus
you lead us
beyond the limits
of winning
and losing.
You move us
from judgment
to acceptance . . .
from brokenness
to blessing.
Your reign
is not a system
of weights and
measures . . .
Your way, instead,
finds balance
through
healing touch.

Draw us
to that place
of peace
when we cannot
penetrate
the wall between
spirit and desire . . .
when pain
prevents us from
making peace
with our past.

While we might not
be able to
forgive . . .
forgive for us.
You know our desire
for homecoming
and healing.
Help us, then,
to open the door
and invite
the holy in. Amen.

The Turning:

What is my motivation for forgiveness? Do I seek permission from God to set limits?

Forgiveness breaks the cycle of resentment.

....

....

....

....

Jesus said to his disciples: "Do not think that I have come to abolish the law and the prophets. I have come, not to abolish them, but to fulfill them" (Mt 5:17).

God
of our fullness,
you do not
cast away the
past
to make room
for today.
Instead,
you desire
that we mold
the flesh
of our actions
according to the
framework
of covenant-love,
a love
built upon
foundations
cast in the
human heart.

Your Word
is the thread
woven
through generations
of promise
and hope.

Old and new
meet in your
solemn oath
of trust and truth.
Alpha and Omega
embrace
in this
Word-made-flesh.

Teach us how
to hold
the thread
long held by
the flesh and blood
of faith,
that we might
weave today
through the rich garment
of yesterday. Amen.

The Turning:

Jesus invites me to develop a sixth sense—a sense of divine providence. It is with this that life will lead me . . . in peace.

Faith is the activity that carries me through my waiting on the Lord.

....

....

....

Jesus was casting out a devil which was mute, and when the devil was cast out the dumb man spoke. The crowds were amazed at this. . . . Others, to test him, were demanding of him a sign from heaven (Lk 11:14, 16).

God of silence,
perhaps what is
mute
within us
is merely
your Word
beyond words.
You call forth
this Word
in Jesus,
who loosens
tongues
to articulate
the meaning
of faithful love.

The light
of daily miracles
casts out
the darkness
and welcomes in
the kingdom . . .
for you join us
in Jesus.

Forgive us
when we resist
your invitation
to accept
the mystery
of your Word.
Enable us to walk
each day
in the shade
of that truth.

Teach us
how to live
with one another.
Do not allow
our lack
of understanding
to be a source
of conflict
but the assurance
of your presence . . .
a presence
beyond our grasp
yet within our reach.
Amen.

The Turning:

How do I respond to the miracles God has worked in my life? Am I a believer?

Choosing to believe rests in the crucial moment between doubt and faith, hesitancy and confidence, control and abandon.

....

....

....

Jesus replied: "... you shall love the Lord your God with all your heart, with all your soul, with all your mind, and with all your strength.... You shall love your neighbor as yourself" (Mk 12: 29–31).

O God,
who is one,
you call us
to yourself
through love.
Life
is the home
of your grace.
Life
is the evidence
of your hope
in us.

You draw us
to yourself
by touching
the places
of blessing
that gift us
to human life.
We now lift
those gifts
to you
with the hope
of holy union ...

Bless our hearts
with love
for you and
one another.
Inspire our spirits
with freedom
and devotion.
Challenge our minds
with truth.
Nourish our strength
with courage.

Focus
our conversion
away from fire
and ashes ...
to the burning
transformation
of action,
that we might
place desire
on the altar
of experience. Amen.

The Turning:

I was born into God—into the inexhaustible mystery of love. I am called to continue that miracle for others.

Jesus does not want me to remain at the foot of the cross. He wants me to return his cross-embrace by loving.

....

....

The Pharisee with head unbowed prayed in this fashion: "I give you thanks, O God, that I am not like the rest... grasping, crooked, adulterous...." The other man, however, kept his distance, not even daring to raise his eyes to heaven. All he did was beat his breast and say, "O God, be merciful to me, a sinner" (Lk 18:11, 13).

God of light,
you penetrate
our secret places,
not with harshness
but with healing.
Yet, we fear
such tenderness,
for our hearts
would be pierced
by the rays
of your truth...
and at times
we stand strong
in self-righteousness...
We applaud
our goodness
and use
comparison
as the stamp
of approval.

You, though,
draw the curtain
on our show
and introduce
a sinner
as your beloved.

Through the stories
of Jesus
you invite us
to an honest heart—
a heart that embraces
limitation and failure
as warmly as
goodness and success.

Help us, then,
to trust that
difference does not
ensure distinction,
and brokenness
can be used
to build the kingdom.
Amen.

The Turning:

The heart of the gospel is transformation. This can only happen when I experience my brokenness and reconcile it with my beauty... in God.

When I enter the presence of Jesus with honesty, I long to admit the "shadows" in my heart ... cast by the light of Christ.

....

....

SUNDAY

Loving the Darkness

For this Sunday midway through Lent, the gospel readings for the three cycles present a dramatic triptych: on one side, the narrative of the man born blind; on the opposite side, the parable of the prodigal son; in the center, the disturbing words of Jesus: "The light came into the world, but men loved darkness rather than light" (Jn 3:19).

It may be hard for us to conceive that anyone would say: "I would rather be blind, thank you" or "It's more fun to be alone and starving in this strange country than to be loved and secure in my father's house." We do, in fact, often prefer the darkness of sin to the light of virtue. We choose to walk in the shadow-world of selfishness and pride. We hide in the dark alleyways of gratification and ease, away from the revealing light of gospel truth. Jesus strips away our self-deception so that we may see the foolishness of so many of our choices.

On our Lenten journey, we try to enter more deeply into the mystery of the death and resurrection of Jesus, in order to appreciate more fully the incredible, unconditional love of our God. It is the light of that love that will enable us to choose truth over falsehood, self-sacrifice over self-serving. This is the perfect time to take to heart more deeply the images of the prodigal son and the all-forgiving father . . . images that teach us how to forgive and how to accept forgiveness. This is how we best express our love of God and neighbor.

GOSPELS: Cycle A—Jn 9:1–41
Cycle B—Jn 3:14–21
Cycle C—Lk 15:1–3, 11–32

God of light
and love,
you set us
free to be found ...
Free to feel
the gaze of God
without guilt—
without the need
to be more than
to "be."

Free to be found ...
Free to feel
the tenderness
which bares
the human heart.
Where defense of
sinfulness
no longer determines
love.
Where protest of
imperfection
no longer protects.

Free to be found ...
Free to accept
the chasm between
creator and creature
as filled
with compassion,
for love saves us
from the tyranny
of ourselves.

But will we be saved?
Can we allow ourselves
to be found?
Will we rest within
the heart of God
without such armor
to dress our souls?

Sackcloth and ashes
throw us
to the ground
year after year, O God.
How might we touch
our truth
written in the dust
and take the hand
that bids us rise? Amen.

Jesus replied, "Unless you people see signs and wonders, you do not believe." "Sir," the royal official pleaded with him, "come down before my child dies." Jesus told him, "Return home. Your son will live." The man put his trust in the word Jesus spoke to him, and started for home (Jn 4:48–50).

God of possibilities,
we look for
proof—
desiring to be
dazzled
by signs and wonders.
You, instead,
seek faith—
calling us
to believe
in your word.
That Word
became flesh
and carried us
beyond promise
to abundant life.

We seek healing
today
in the gift
of faith
that leads us
down the road
to Jesus.
Faith
that casts out
fear.
Faith that
opens the door
to hope.

Pour this gift
of faith,
O God,
into hearts broken
by cynicism-yet-need.
Let the sign
of this weakness
be the place
that bears the seal
of your love. Amen.

The Turning:

Abraham, the father of faith, left everything he held dear ... based not on what he saw but on the word of God.

Instead of longing to believe, I must pray in order to believe. Belief is the choice I make between meaninglessness and mystery.

....

....

....

Jesus said, "Do you want to be healed?" "Sir," the sick man answered, "I don't have anyone to plunge me into the pool once the water has been stirred up" (Jn 5:6–8).

God of healing,
we come to you
in pieces
at times—
unable to hear
your word,
walk in your ways,
hope for what
is beyond
the human eye.

We desire healing
but know that
by ourselves
we are unable
to risk freedom's leap
into your
waiting arms.
Have mercy, then,
and lift us.

Carry us,
O God,
more deeply
into the waters
of our baptism.
Drown us in grace,
that we may
have life
through the breath
of your Spirit.

Keep us willing
in hope . . .
care-free
in faith . . .
waiting on love. Amen.

The Turning:

Grace meets me on the road and leads me to Jesus—the miracle of my healing.

To experience my weakness, yet to realize acceptance, leads to healing . . . for God is not discouraged with me even when I am discouraged with myself.

....
....
....
....
....

This was Jesus' answer: "I solemnly assure you, the Son cannot do anything by himself—he can do only what he sees the Father doing" (Jn 5:19).

O God,
who is father
and mother,
who holds us
warmly
in a parent's
love ...
today we desire
to draw upon
the bountiful
legacy
of that love.
Our brother, Jesus,
understood
the richness
of this relationship.
He lived
under the blessing
of belonging
to you.

Your love
lets go
and allows us
to choose
the places
where we may
grow.
But sometimes
we lack
right judgment.
It is then
we look to you
and ask
for a will
in keeping with
our desires.

Give us the
mind of Christ
which was fashioned
by the Spirit,
and a heart
which knows
the loving wisdom
of your will. Amen.

The Turning:

To be created in the image and likeness of God is both glory and burden. God never intended to discourage me, but to challenge me.

The incarnation is the divine embrace of human limitation.

....

....

....

Jesus said to the Jews: "He [John] was the lamp, set aflame and burning bright, and for a while you exulted willingly in his light. Yet I have testimony greater than John's. . . . I have come in my Father's name, yet you do not accept me" (Jn 5:35–36, 43).

God of unbelievers,
we want to
believe,
but it is hard
for us to trust
what we do not
see.
You knew that need
and so embraced
our unbelief in
Jesus,
who sought sinners
and loved us
into truth.

Give us, then,
the love
of your Christ
who clothed
his words in
flesh.

The courage
of your Christ,
who raised
the burning lamp
of John
to light the horizon
of life itself.

The faith
of your Christ,
who poured himself
into the chalice
of human suffering
to shatter its darkness
forever.

O God,
fill us with faith
that will carry us
beyond the waters
of our baptism
that we, too,
may be love,
light and life. Amen.

The Turning:

Faith is a gift, not because some receive it and others do not . . . but because God gives faith freely. I do not occasion the gift.

Faith lives in the quiet corners of desire.

....
....
....
....

Jesus moved about within Galilee ... because some of the Jews were looking for a chance to kill him. The Jewish feast of Booths drew near. Once his brothers had gone up to the festival he too went up, but as if in secret and not for all to see (Jn 7:1–2, 10).

God of time,
you teach us
to respect the hour,
the moment ...
for epiphany
might go unnoticed
if we were not
to watch for stars.

For Jesus
time was sacred—
not to be rushed
yet
not to be denied
in the face
of its birth.

With Jesus,
may we live
in this rhythm
of breath-by-breath
and freely
ride the pendulum
to yet another grace.

Save us from fear
that would
make time captive,
causing us
to cling to the fruit
long after the ripening.

Teach us
to hold the moment
lightly,
that we might not
impose upon it
meaning it holds not.

May we recognize
each day
as opportunity,
be moved
by the color-cry
of dawn
and greet the grace
that time
hopes for us. Amen.

The Turning:

It is true—I may not know the day nor the hour—but I need not be afraid. What began with a loving God will be completed ... fulfilled ... embraced by my loving God.

Do I ask, "What is around me to keep me safe?" or "Who is within me?"

....

....

"Surely the Messiah is not to come from Galilee? Does not scripture say that the Messiah, being of David's family is to come from Bethlehem, the village where David lived?" In this fashion the crowd was sharply divided over him [Jesus] (Jn 7:41–43).

O God,
forever free
of our theories
and ideas,
you challenge
the limits we place
on you . . .
in the person
of Jesus.

There,
you are not
to be grasped.
Instead,
we are invited
to dream dreams
and seek
possibilities,
for
life leads us
to Jesus.
And
what we seek
can be found.

Protect us
from the blindness
of cynicism.
Give us vision
that permits
decisions
of the heart.

Continue
to elude us
when defining you
is only for comfort.
Our minds,
for all their wonder,
can build enclosures
that trap
creative-joy.

Let us lift
the gift
of your presence
free of our attachments,
and rise
to the surprise
of grace. Amen.

The Turning:

Doubt is like a storm that must rage its course. The quiet will come, but only after the winds of grace have set my soul free.

The fire of the Holy Spirit purifies my vision so that I clearly see that God is mystery!

....

....

....

SUNDAY

Rising Again

When we come face to face with sin and death, we tend to lose sight of the presence of God. In those frightening moments when we are brought low by human frailty or stand helpless as life ebbs away, it is so hard for us to believe the promise of Jesus to lift us to newness of life.

Yet, this paradox of life-giving death lies at the very heart of the gospel. On various occasions, Jesus spoke about saving one's life by losing it. He agonized over the prospect of his own crucifixion and death, but had unwavering trust that his Father's love and power would bring victory out of apparent defeat. That trust gave him incredible strength and endurance, and sustained him through Good Friday to Easter Sunday.

Our limited vision so often lets us see only our vulnerability and our limitations. We panic! We are overwhelmed and terrified by a sense that the Lord has abandoned us or has turned a deaf ear. And so, quickly we utter a cry of complaint and near despair: "Lord, if only you had been here . . ."

These are the times when we need to recall the image of Jesus summoning Lazarus back to life, and the sinful woman back to integrity and peace. Whenever we are brought low by physical or spiritual infirmity, we must believe in resurrection. We must know that the risen Lord who lives on in us will always call us forth from the tombs of fear and despondency which threaten to bury us.

He will call us forth to new life, again and again and again. Then, one final time, he will call us from earthly death to life eternal. Never again will we utter the lament: "If only you had been here . . ."

GOSPELS: Cycle A—Jn 11:1–45
                Cycle B—Jn 12:20–33
                Cycle C—Jn 8:1–11

Out of the depths
we cry to you, O God,
out of the depths
of our doubt and
disbelief ...
the depths
of our fears
and vulnerability ...
the depths
of the tomb
we carve
into the fabric
of our lives ...
Bound
like Lazarus.
Wrapped in darkness
like a seed.

The words of Jesus
echo in our ears:
to die is to live,
to lose is to find.

Cradle the seed
of our lives
in your hand, O God.
Help us to befriend
the holy ground
of life
that we might not
resist the plunge
into its darkness.

Let us fall lightly
that we might
greet the dying
with the certainty
of new life.

Let us remember
your time in the tomb
but also that
you come
sure as dawn
to shatter the stone
and call us forth
unbound and free. Amen.

Jesus . . . said to her, "Woman where did they all disappear to? Has no one condemned you? "No one, sir," she answered. Jesus said, "Nor do I condemn you. You may go. But from now on, avoid this sin" (Jn 8:10–11).

O God,
who finds us
hiding
in our shadows,
through Jesus
you extend a hand
of hope
inviting us
to step into your
revealing light—
a light
that anoints wounds
long hidden
by fear and shame.

We resist those
who bind
and drag us
from darkness into day,
for their
harshness throws us
at the feet
of judgment.

You
trace words of light
upon our hearts.
Lead us, then,
by love
that we may find
the treasure
of ourselves,
that we may
lift it before
the eyes of Christ
and with him say:
holy . . . holy . . . holy. Amen.

The Turning:

I must gather the past and broken things, and see them as life-builders for today.

I must pray to be a gift to myself, instead of a burden. I must pray to discover and know I am that gift.

....

....

....

....

....

....

"Who are you then?" they asked him. Jesus answered: "What I have been telling you from the beginning.... When you lift up the Son of Man, you will come to realize that I AM and that I do nothing by myself. I say only what the Father has taught me" (Jn 8:25, 28).

God of patience,
we often come
before you
seeking answers
already wrapped
within your Word.

The untiring heart
of Jesus
holds our questions
until
faith finds us
willing
to walk beyond
our needs.

With Jesus our God,
we climb the wood,
open our arms
and outstretch our feet.

We welcome
the flow of water
and blood—
longing
to be washed
in Spirit and in Truth.

May the source
of our lives
and the healer
of our souls
embrace us
in his final
sigh...
for that moment,
his last breath,
stirred
the first breath
of our lives. Amen.

The Turning:

Jesus left us the legacy of the cross. Many times I see myself carrying the cross. And yet, the cross can also carry me...in the power of the resurrection.

To be a disciple means to accept the suffering along the way—to engage it. The result is transformation...not destruction.

....

....

....

....

Jesus said to those Jews who believed in him: "If you live accord-ing to my teaching, you are truly my disciples; then you will know the truth and the truth will set you free." "We are de-scendants of Abraham," was their answer. "Never have we been slaves to anyone. What do you mean by saying, 'You will be free'?" (Jn 8:31–32).

God of courage,
we anticipate
your Spirit
in the words
of Jesus, today.
Freedom and truth
kiss the fire
of life.
But fear
fires obstinate hearts,
and words of life
are unmet sparks.

Help us
to lift fear
from our shoulders
and throw it
off the edges
of this earth.
Let it fall
into its own orbit,
perhaps encircling us

but never again
crashing down and
crushing us to
unbelief.

Your truth
does not teach
with violence.
Your freedom
intends to heal.

Be with us, O God.
Help us
cast out fear
by love, by grace . . .
by you.
Lift us
out of the depths
of our unknown
thirsts
into the fullness
of freedom and life. Amen.

The Turning:

The mystery of God's presence within me abides with my ques-tions, and softens the cutting-edge of my fears.

To know God in pain? Yes! God is held captive by the struggle of the human heart.

....
....
....

Jesus answered, ". . . Very truly, I tell you, whoever keeps my word will never see death" (Jn 8:51, NRSV).

God of the living,
your Word spoke
life—
preparing the earth
for humankind.
This Word, spoken
again and again
in Jesus,
parted the veil
of time
that we might
know beyond
our wildest dreams.

But will we ever
comprehend
new life?
Will death forever
be the mystery
that blurs our vision,
preventing us
from fathoming life's
fullness?

Let the wideness
of your mercy
be upon us, O God.
Receive our questions.
Give us courage
to walk with them
into eternal day.

When fear
frightens us,
call us to the feet
of your
Word-made-flesh
and there
set us free.

Call us forth
unbound
that we may leave
the tomb
of our terrors
with hope
in resurrected life. Amen.

The Turning:

Where do I taste death and long for new life? Wherever it is, it is precisely there that Jesus says: "Come forth!"

As life slowly leaves me, there is a birth taking place. . . . I pass through the door of promise and am born of God.

....

....

....

....

....

"It is not for any 'good deed' that we are stoning you," the Jews retorted, "but for blaspheming. You who are only a man are making yourself God." Jesus answered: "... If I do not perform my Father's works, put no faith in me. But if I do perform them ... put faith in these works, so as to realize ... the Father is in me and I in him." At these words they again tried to arrest him, but he eluded their grasp (Jn 10:33, 37–39).

O God,
your
   Word-made-flesh
shattered our notions
of messiah
and challenged our
concept of the
   kingdom.
Jesus
held your face
before us
and smiled ...
but longing
   prohibited
the possibility
of a gentle God ...
or a heart's desire
come true.

The wrappings of
Mystery,
meant to draw us
   near,
became a cloak
for cynicism and
disbelief, instead.
Many walked away
praying for the
dreamer ...
the blasphemer.

O God,
slow our steps.
Do not allow us
to walk away from
your Son.
When his truth
falls hard
upon our hearts,

help us to find
the impossible
possible.
Let us reach
the heights
of your Spirit
that we may
descend, willingly,
into the Mystery
that wraps us round
in love.

May we proclaim
kinship in Christ
and your presence
in him ...
the final Word
of love. Amen.

The Turning:

When I pray that God may show me the way, do I sometimes miss the person or situation that God provides?

Finding God makes certain demands upon me, yet that "knowing" empowers me to meet the challenge.

....

....

....

...[T]he Pharisees called a meeting of the Sanhedrin. "What are we to do," they said.... "If we let him go on like this, the whole world will believe in him."... From that day onward there was a plan afoot to kill him. (Jn 11:47–48, 53)

God of the prophets,
Jesus
was the lamb
of sacrifice
whose blood sealed
your covenant
love,
because
fear generated
disbelief
when wonder and
forgiveness flowed.

Thoughts of destruction
hung heavy
in the air
when mystery
could not be grasped.
Deceit
worked its way
into the human heart—
killing
what it did not
comprehend.

Forgive us our fears,
today,
when we use them
to choose rejection
of your miracle-Son.
His abandon
to our imperfection
argues against
our notions of self
which challenge
such love.

Do not let us
destroy
your dedication
of grace
because of jealousy,
bitterness or pride.

Fill our flesh
with the fullness
of the Spirit
that faith
may lead us
beyond ourselves
to the blessings
of our unknowing. Amen.

The Turning:

I am weak, but do I accept my weakness? I am poor, but do I accept my poverty? Real change is born of acceptance.

It is a flash of God-light that changes blindness into blessing.

....

....

....

PASSION SUNDAY

Jesus, you embraced abandonment
by those who called you Teacher and Lord
and accepted the cross
without question or condemnation.
May we embrace those who
no longer have need for us...
those who leave our lives.
MAY WE EMBRACE THEM IN PEACE.

Jesus, you surrendered to ignorance,
humiliation and injustice.
May we surrender our need for approval
and understanding.
MAY WE SURRENDER THESE NEEDS IN PEACE.

Jesus, you raised your arms to heaven willingly,
accepting death as a way to truth and life.
May we lower our demands on one another
and accept the God of love
as image and likeness of you.
MAY WE SEEK THIS DEEPER TRUTH IN PEACE.

Jesus, you died alone, hanging against the sky,
crying out... fearing the Father had forgotten you.
May we cry out with love
when fear and isolation threaten our lives.
MAY WE DARE TO LOVE IN PEACE.

Jesus, in the end, bowing your head,
you gave over your body and spirit
to the God you could not see.
Savior and Lord, in the end
may we bow our human minds to divine wisdom,
give our bodies to sacrificial love
and place our spirits in holy union with you...
our act of faith in the God we cannot see.
BLESS US, O LORD, WITH PEACE. AMEN.

MONDAY

Mary brought a pound of costly perfume ... with which she anointed Jesus' feet. Then she dried his feet with her hair. ... Jesus replied: "Leave her alone. Let her keep it against the day they prepare me for burial" (Jn 12:3–8).

The Turning:

Death is the door to the promise of always "being." It is not an empty moment, rather it is full . . . the glory to be revealed as capacity for God.

I face death much like a major seventh chord seeking resolution, for death is the threshold experience to resolution, to God.

Perhaps I need to know longing so that I can rejoice in fulfillment.

The dust I was created from and the ashes to which I will return are sanctuary for the breath of life.

God loved me to death. If I remember love to the point of death, I must also remember life through death . . . to the point of resurrection.

I am able to face the mystery of my mortality with hope because resurrection happens each time I hand myself over.

The sleep of death has healing powers which restore us to life anew.

In eternity God continues to love me into perfection/wholeness. Purgatory is divine love, not divine wrath.

When I am finally called home, will God be able to say, "I know in whom I have believed"?

....

....

....

....

....

....

....

....

....

TUESDAY

"Lord," Peter said to him, *"...I will lay down my life for you!"* *"You will lay down your life for me, will you?"* Jesus answered. *"I tell you truly, the cock will not crow before you have three times disowned me!"* (Jn 13:37–38).

The Turning:

My weakness is an opportunity to encounter grace.

The banquet of salvation will be attended by some, perhaps many, unexpected guests.

The truth of God and the truth of myself: I am totally dependent, yet God is totally dependable.

I am forgiven, at times, without my knowing. I must leave the past behind.

Jesus endured humiliation, injustice, pain and death. He loved me with a passion.

Jesus chose earth for heaven, meekness for power, vulnerability for strength, the cross for glory, and said, "Come, follow me!"

Discipleship sees brokenness as opportunity—opportunity to celebrate grace.

When I pray for healing, am I willing to commit myself to that new way of life?

I must live my brokenness under the blessing of God.

....

....

....

....

....

....

....

....

....

....

....

... Judas ... said, "What are you willing to give me if I hand him over to you?" They paid him thirty pieces of silver, and from that time on he kept looking for an opportunity to hand him [Jesus] over (Mt 26:15–16).

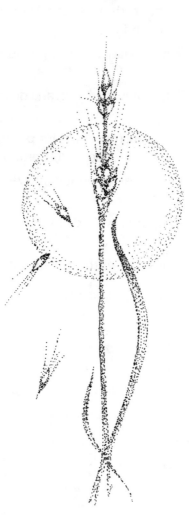

The Turning:

"Father, forgive them. . . . " For Jesus, this moment was an act of faith—faith in the power of light over darkness.

When I pray for peace that the world cannot give, I must remember it is also a peace that the world cannot take away.

I must abandon my need for security and my fears for survival. Only then will I experience trust—the freedom of the resurrection.

The grain of wheat must willingly fall to the ground . . .

I must be open to the grace of powerlessness. . . . Choose it in all its fearfulness for it is strength when joined with Jesus.

If the crucifixion was part of Jesus' life, it will be part of mine as well. The experience of the cross does not make God's love for me any less.

By his stripes we are healed. Each time I embrace the wounds of the whip, I meet the place of my healing.

For Jesus, it is finished. For me, it has just begun.

....

....

....

....

....

....

....

....

....

....

....

HOLY THURSDAY

This supper hour holds feast and famine ...
Teeth will tear at flesh, devouring the lamb.
We gather to celebrate fullness.
We gather to weep at bones numbered
and placed in hollow rock.

Towel and water pass on bended knee—
A servant song is chanted as pride lowers its head
and charity becomes Teacher and Lord.

Tears are dried with bread broke open and shared.
Such power in a grain of wheat.
Living in darkness prepared for this feast.
Yet death's stone must greet the seed
and break it into fullness.
Blood wine passes lip to lip,
flooding new life with sacrifice.
The bell of remembering tolls with rhythm
and tone, heavy on the human heart.

Father, this meal,
  my last supper—
  I feel it in my bones.
  My flesh prepares
  a three-day fast.

Doom weights heavy on me, now.
  and yet,
  I am called to remember
  a passing-over.
  I am called to celebrate
  slavery and freedom.

My friends prepare
  a table for me
  in the sight of
  all my foes.

Father,
  I close my eyes
  and see within
  the end of my journey.
  So soon, Father,
  so soon?

I know they are gathering now
  in the streets
  outside our dinner-room.
  I know, Father, I know.

But, one more thing—
  just one more
  passing-on before
  the passing-over.

I go now to celebrate
  your love for us.
  I go to remember
  the gift
  and to become
  the gift.

I go to pass over
  from slavery to freedom
  TODAY.
I go to share food
  and become bread.
I go to declare that
  the chains of bondage
  are broken.
I go to become broken.

FATHER, WILL THEY REMEMBER
  ME?

Your will be done, Father ...
  and be there with me
  in the doing. Amen.

GOOD FRIDAY

A garden awaits... more tears, more blood.
The body prepares itself for breaking.
Friends await with desires and dreams.
Then conflict explodes...
Spirit and flesh kiss their reality
in fear, in anger, in terror...
in denial.
Truth is tossed about in search of understanding.
Justice is surprised with cries of hatred.
Wood weighs heavy.
Anguish tumbles forth from eyes
that are left with only seeing.

Finally... flesh is pierced
and kinship is confirmed in thief and mother.
Then with arms raised and open
Spirit-breath heaves a sigh
and life surrenders life.
Later, only later... love cradles love
and brings her womb's joy to rest.

Death is all around me.
  Father, have you forsaken me?
  Have they?

How can I reach
  through the door of death
  and touch you
  on the other side?
How can I shake hands,
  hold hands, enfold hands
  with those
  who walked through
  before me?

I thirst . . .
  are you enough
  to quench my need?

You are source
  and satisfaction.
  How does that
  plumb the depths
  of my well, today?

My bones are numbered,
  dry and brittle
  each time I hang
  from this cross.
I die many times
  see the hope,
  but die again and again.

When I commend my spirit,
  at the end,
  will you be there
  to catch and capture it?
How will I sink into
  the inexhaustible mystery
  of you?

If you are love,
  and we meet on the other
    side—
  will I keep loving?
Will this new flesh
  reach into you?
  And back across to the other
    side?

Will I continue
  to co-create, to build
  the kingdom, to rescue
  the poor, to lift up hearts,
  to affect life,
  to effect life,
  to touch the earth?

What history do I hold
  in my heart now?
  Who has been reaching
  back to me through time?

    . . . MANY I THINK . . .

Father, into your hands
I commend my spirit—
and join THEM in this giving.
Amen.

Holy Night . . .

Holy Light,
burn deeply
in my soul.
Hallow the tomb
of my flesh
that freedom
may laugh
where bondage
once wept.

Holy Night . . .

Holy Light,
pour
your healing word,
the Yes-of-God,
into wounds
left dark and deep—
aching with desire
for this anointing.

Holy Night . . .

Holy Light,
cast rays of grace
into my night.
Let them
seek the corners
of my heart
where hides
the fear of my
shadowland.

Holy Night . . .

Holy Light,
carry me
across the threshold
of joy-at-dawn,
that day will find
love
leading me
to life. Amen.

The Resurrection
of
Our Lord

Laughter echoes in the tomb,
fills the hollows
and rolls away the stone
that separates the heart
of humankind
from the heart of God.

The song of birds
greets the laughter—
blends with it
and plays with the melody
of joy in the morning.

Wrappings of yesterday
are left as memories,
reminders of what was . . .
and what will be
for us.
But empty grave and
open doorway
hold the laughter
that will follow—
for we, too,
will leave yesterday
behind.

Touch . . . and Believe!

Like Thomas, we find death easy to believe in, but resurrection questionable. Dying is very physical and tangible. But rising from the dead challenges the testimony of our senses. Thomas remembered vividly his master's last hours—the blood, the nails, the cry of agony, and the entombment. When he hears the others proclaim: "He is risen!" he needs and wants physical reassurance. He needs to touch scars on the hands and feet of a body that has been raised up. Then he will believe.

We are all too familiar with the trappings of death. Too often, we are witnesses to the dying of our loved ones. We see the diminishment of the body, feel the pain, and hear the labored breathing. We experience the finality, the mute coldness, the sad rites of passage, then the absence and the emptiness. All this cries out "the end"—while the voice of faith shouts: "A new beginning!"

The Lord certainly understands our anguish and our doubts . . . and our need to touch the mystery of resurrection. Our baptismal faith makes that possible. It enables us to move beyond the realm of the senses to live in the awareness of his radiant, risen presence. There, we can hear him say: "Touch me, and believe!"

In prayer, and especially at the eucharist, we walk in the company of the Easter Lord. New life radiates from him, giving us the power to transform defeat into victory, sorrow into joy, and doubt into joyful hope. To claim that we are "resurrection people" is not just poetic license; it describes the reality of authentic Christian living. We will only enter that reality when, like Thomas, we have reached out in faith, touched the risen Christ, and proclaimed: "My Lord and my God!"

GOSPELS: All Cycles—Jn 20:19–31

O God,
in you darkness
and light
are the same.
I pray you, then,
abide with me
in the shadows.
Become the cloak
of darkness
that wraps my
steps.

Mantle
my movements
that frustration
and fear
might not harm
me
in this journey
of night ...
for doubt
drags
my feet
and questions
disquiet
my soul.

Jesus,
my resurrection
and life,
let my blindness
not hide me
from you.
Rather
redeem the darkness
I live.
Transform
this stumbling block
of doubt
into
a stepping stone
of strength
that I may walk
on the waters
of my baptism.

Uphold my steps
by faith.
Guide my heart
through hope.
Consecrate my path
with love.

May my
death to light
be the birth
of soul-fire
that leads me to you. Amen.

SUNDAY

Do You Love Me?

The resurrection appearances of Jesus are filled with surprises. He breaks out of a sealed tomb, appears through locked doors, breaks bread, eats fish, asks for faith, commitment and love. He is forgiving of denial, patient with doubt, supportive of weakness, eager for loyalty. He seeks more than just acceptance of his having overcome death; he asks for intimacy: "Do you love me?"

The risen Lord is anxious to repair relationships—with Mary Magdalene, with the two disciples returning to Emmaus, with each of the apostles, but most of all with Peter. He assures all of forgiveness, but wants reconciliation to nurture even greater personal bonds. To each and all, he asks: "Do you love me?"

Each of us struggles to believe in Jesus, to be faithful to him. But we are so slow to understand, quick to deny, strong with words, but weak with actions. We are so often unwilling to pay the price of discipleship. Yet we always hang in; we are always willing to try one more time. We trust in his patience and compassion, and know that he is ever ready to forgive, to heal, to lead us to greater maturity and more perfect fidelity.

The disciples of Emmaus recognized the risen Lord in the breaking of the bread. Ever since the last supper, the followers of Jesus have grown in intimacy with him at the table of the eucharist. There he becomes our food, our sustenance, our very life. There he gives himself to us, and we give ourselves to him. There, like Peter, we can assure him most sincerely: "Lord, you know all things; you know that I love you." And he will continue to invite us to follow him, promising to sustain us through the difficult times, the hardships, the rejections, the trials, the crucifixions, leading us always to resurrection.

GOSPELS: Cycle A—Lk 24:13–35
Cycle B—Lk 24:35–48
Cycle C—Jn 21:1–19

Will I recognize
you, O Lord,
in broken bread,
in realities harsh
and
dreams that remain
only dreams?

At those moments
when terror
fills my heart,
touch
the scars of
lost hope...
then shattered spirits
will be healed;
for
I, too,
hold bread
to break the grace
of each day.

Help me...
to walk with strangers;
to allow them
to unfold
the good news of life;
to cradle another's
pain
in my heart;
to feed the
hunger
of unmet needs.

I walk to Emmaus
again and again
trusting
that you join me
on the journey.
With you as
companion and guide
I, too, will become
a giver of grace. Amen.

SUNDAY

Shepherds All

In our day, the imagery of shepherd and sheep would seem very foreign to those who lead and to those who are led. Leadership so often manifests itself in terms of power and control; it can easily become oppressive and insensitive. Jesus deliberately chose a very pastoral image to describe his relationship with his followers. His authority would always be loving and gentle. He would invite, not command. He would lead to security and freedom, not to some form of blind obedience and slavery.

We cherish the image of Jesus as the "good shepherd," because it assures us that he knows us by name, seeks us out when we stray, and wards off those who would attack or injure us. His way leads to "green pastures" of goodness and happiness. In his company, we will find shelter and rest.

Our role as followers, however, cannot be self-centered and passive. If we understand the gospel message, we know that Jesus invites us to share his shepherding. As Christians we are called to manifest his kind of gentle concern for others. We cannot be indifferent when we see people who are hurting, or lost, or in danger. We might be tempted to turn away, to disclaim responsibility, or to wait for someone else to respond—but the voice of the good shepherd speaks to our conscience: "I lay down my life for my sheep—but the hired hand . . . runs away."

Once we have experienced the gentle concern and compassion of the Lord, it is unthinkable for us to reject the ministry of shepherding. Our eyes become his, searching for the lost sheep; our hands and hearts become instruments of his love and service. The good shepherd can reach out to all when we are all good shepherds.

GOSPELS: Cycle A—Jn 10:1–10
Cycle B—Jn 10:11–18
Cycle C—Jn 10:27–30

The Lord is my light
who fills and floods
the darkness within
and without.
I shall not fear.

Light leads me
to possibilities
where I step
the dance of hope.

The path to life
opens out before me
as light illumines
the way.
Even when night falls
I do not hesitate,
for the presence
of light
sharpens my vision
beyond the powers
of sight.

Abundance greets me
despite the hungers
of every day...
Light sustains me
and threads me through
the shadows of harm.

Goodness and love
are guests
at my table,
for light empties
the chairs
of foreboding and fear.

Forever I will dwell
in the temple
of light
and there
celebrate my need.
For there, in light,
I will unfold
the places
yet to be filled
and freed. Amen.

SUNDAY

Show Me!

Philip asks, in the name of all searchers, "Show us the Father, and it is enough." With the simplicity of "one in whom there is no guile" the disciple asks the Lord to lay open before his eyes the ineffable mystery of the transcendent divinity. Jesus answers: "Whoever has seen me has seen the Father." In that cryptic sentence is revealed the wonder of the incarnation!

As incredible as it may seem, in Jesus the love, compassion and power of God take on flesh and blood. The entire Jesus story has one theme: "Let me tell you about my Father!" Each circumstance of his life becomes a piece of the mosaic that ultimately depicts for us the image of God. In the relationships, incidents and parables of that life the mystery of God is translated into the language of our humanity. How much more intimately could the almighty be united with us? How could he manifest his love for us any more personally or convincingly? As an answer to all who ask: "Show us the Father," Jesus is more than enough.

Doubt and skepticism, however, continue to plague the believer and the non-believer. The gift of Jesus strikes many as almost too good to be true. Somehow, they find it more acceptable to keep imaging God as one who is remote, unconcerned and insensitive. The "will of God" hangs over them as a cold and immutable arbiter of human affairs. This can lead to discouragement and despair.

The God who made us in the divine image knows well how frail and vulnerable we can be. And so he sends his Son into our world to show us how to live with a sense of God's nearness and concern in the ordinary and extraordinary events of our lives. Thus we can enjoy the freedom, hope and joy befitting the children of a loving and compassionate creator.

GOSPELS: Cycle A—Jn 14:1–12
Cycle B—Jn 15:1–8
Cycle C—Jn 13:31–33a, 34–35

God of growing things,
you gave us
Jesus
as the vine
of our existence.
Hold me firm, then,
to his ways.
Draw me deeply
down
into the ground
of love
where you are
rooted
in the human heart.

May the air
I breathe
be charged with
charity,
the life
of his creative
energy—
the truth
that will set me
free
of selfish concern.

Lift me
from the earth
of my ego-dwelling.
Fix faith
in my soul
that will hold
me fast . . .
for life
may lead me
to places
I do not wish
to go.

Cast the memory
of Jesus
as bread
along my way.
Then,
what I fear
as mere crumbs
becomes
a banquet—
a wisdom of heart
. . . the cost of loving.
Amen.

SUNDAY

That Your Joy May Be Complete

John remembers the last hours of Jesus—the supper, the washing of feet, and the final discourse. There was an ominous sense that great sorrow was about to overwhelm them, and that their master and friend was about to leave them. But there was also a promise that they would never be alone, because he would pour out his Spirit upon them. What John remembered most vividly was the reassurance that this gift of the Spirit would bring about a new kind of personal intimacy with him and the fullness of joy.

Certainly, Jesus makes it clear that, if we choose to become his disciples, we must be ready and willing to take up our cross daily. We know that in baptism we have entered into the mystery of his death. So we might conclude that the characteristic mood of the faithful Christian should be one of somber resignation to suffering. But, on the eve of his own death, the Lord promises that, when we, too, have his Spirit poured out upon us, his joy will be in us and our joy will be complete.

A profound and abiding sense of joy is the hallmark of a person whose faith in Jesus is authentic. This does not mean some sort of superficial and momentary happiness. Nor does it imply an attitude of escapism from the presence of pain and suffering in human experience. But it does mean that our trust in God is not shaken in the face of evil. We are always aware of the indwelling of the Spirit that permeates our minds and hearts with joy. That joy generates strength and hope, courage and peace.

GOSPELS: Cycle A—Jn 14:15–21
Cycle B—Jn 15:9–17
Cycle C—Jn 14:23–29

Spirit
of the promise,
lead me
on life's journey
that I may find
wisdom of heart,
for
it was love
that led Jesus
to the sacred place
of humankind.
It was love
that led Jesus
from the desert
to the cross.
There
in the desert,
death and life . . .
I meet you.

Lift the blindness
from my heart.
Awaken the silence
of my soul
to the joyful
celebration
of your life within.

Tear down the
walls
which separate me
from others,
that I may
come to see the
face of God
reflected
in their eyes.

Spirit of holiness,
flood me with
freedom
that I may become
the fire that seals
this covenant-love.

Heal my spirit
that I may
walk this earth
as a pilgrim—
creating the kingdom
I hold
in my heart. Amen.

ASCENSION OF OUR LORD

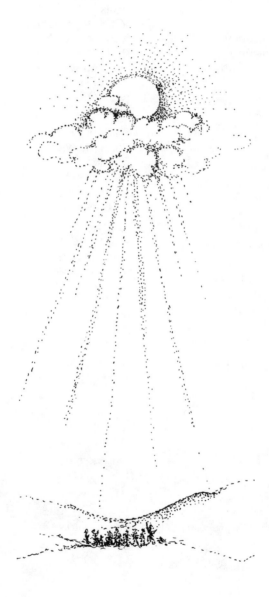

Jesus,
I know you had
to leave us,
but to this day
I wish the presence
I miss.
I stand with your disciples
looking up and around . . .
for you.

Sometimes I am unclear
of my direction
in this kingdom on earth.
Yet angel-words ring
in my ears and call me
to rise to the responsibility
of becoming the reflected
Christ.

Nostalgia is not necessary
for your nearness.
Dreams of former days
become the hope of today
and the reality of tomorrow.

Move me to this mission
of yours.
Provide me with the memories
of your life
that will fire my movement
of change . . . with justice,
with love.

Let me celebrate your Spirit
by living the vision
of prism-grace
which blesses the many edges
of life . . .
and seals my soul
for your return. Amen.

SUNDAY

That All May Be One

In the final unburdening of his heart, Jesus prays in a very loving, intimate way for those special friends to whom he is entrusting his mission. But his prayer looks far beyond these first disciples. His thirst is for faith; he wants future generations to accept him as Lord and Savior, as the full and final revelation of the Father's love. But he knows that it will not be his message or his miracles that will ultimately engender this kind of faith. Only when the lives of his followers project a unique and genuine oneness will their witness be authentic and compelling.

Jesus prays that those who choose to become his disciples will put aside all divisive and exclusive attitudes of mind and heart. As they come to understand and live his gospel, they must accept one another as brothers and sisters, regardless of differences in age, race and condition. They must rise above all prejudice and bias. They must manifest heartfelt concern for one another's needs and hurts. Those who look from outside the community must be able to say, with wonder, "See how these Christians love one another!"

There are profound implications in this prayer of Jesus for unity. Whenever we who claim to be his followers fail in any way to be fully one with each other, we jeopardize the credibility of the gospel. If our commitment to unity is half-hearted, or if our faith communities are not totally inclusive, in every way, we fall short of the ideal that Jesus insists must be the hallmark of his church.

GOSPELS: Cycle A—Jn 17:1–11a
Cycle B—Jn 17:11b–19
Cycle C—Jn 17:20–26

God of my heart,
in the hour
of surrender
Jesus offered a
legacy
tender in prayer.
Filled with anticipation
he held us
with hope and
thanksgiving
and begged for us
full share
in the mystery.

God of my heart,
give me the humility
to surrender,
for my prayer
is often
an act of faith—
believing
without seeing,
trusting
without knowing,
loving
without feeling.

God of my heart,
yesterday and tomorrow
lie in balance.
May I not
measure myself
by the past
nor
fracture myself
by the future.
Lord of all
that makes me
me,
keep me from
burdening others
with my ideals.
Gift me
with your words
but teach me
how to listen.

And when I come
to the edge
of this life
throw open the doors
to my deepest desire
and bid me fly
into your fullness...
O God of my heart. Amen.

The disciples said to Jesus: "At last you are speaking plainly without talking in veiled language.... We do indeed believe you came from God" (Jn 16:29–30).

PRAYER TO THE HOLY SPIRIT

Spirit of God—
soothing breath within
that heals in its
passing through ...
until jagged spaces
are polished smooth
and puzzle pieces
touch to wholeness.

COME, BREATH OF GOD!

Reflection:

God breathed me to life.... I am held in this rapture of image and likeness.

I am the story of God ... a story of love, grace and healing. God's word is without limits!

....
....
....
....
....
....
....
....
....

Jesus looked up to heaven and said: "Father, the hour has come! Give glory to your Son that your Son may give glory to you" (Jn 17:1).

PRAYER TO THE HOLY SPIRIT

Spirit of God—
winds that whirl
and swirl
in apparent storm;
breaking apart
our houses
of complacency and
stagnation;
destroying our towers
of preconceived
notions
held by egos
who have lost sight
of your truth . . .
their truth . . .
the I AM.

COME, WINDS OF CHANGE!

Reflection:

As I forgive, accept and love myself, I come to know God . . . for I can only come to know the God of my experience.

Is it change that makes me different, or what I bring to that change?

....

....

....

"... O Father most holy, protect them with the name you have given me ... guard them from the evil one. ... Consecrate them by means of truth" (Jn 17:11, 15, 17).

PRAYER TO THE HOLY SPIRIT

Spirit of God—
gentle touch that lifts
the bruised reed
and embraces
the fearful heart ...
inviting
the return of life
and the courage
to be;
restoring integrity
and self-generation.

COME, TOUCH OF LIFE!

Reflection:

Jesus says to the child within, "Come forth!"

God calls me to holiness, but the perfection God seeks is wholeness.

....

....

....

....

....

....

....

....

*". . . that all may be one as you, Father, are in me, and I in you;
I pray that they may be [one] in us . . ." (Jn 17:21).*

PRAYER TO THE HOLY SPIRIT

Spirit of God—
Wisdom
beyond our understanding.
Desire
that draws us
yet eludes
our total grasp.
Gift
precious to our hearts
and vital
to our lives.
Author
of visions and dreams.
Source
of who we are . . .
Goal
of who we will become . . .
union with our God.

COME, HOLY WISDOM!

Reflection:

I sustain a "single-heart" by a vision that penetrates life through
the eyes of God.

God is my Center . . . source and resource.

....

....

....

"Simon, son of John, do you love me?" . . . He [Peter] said to him:
"Lord, you know everything. You know well that I love you." Jesus
told him, "Feed my sheep" (Jn 21:17).

PRAYER TO THE HOLY SPIRIT

Spirit of God—
energy of love
that raptures and
captures
the human heart . . .
drawing us to all
that is holy—
to one another,
to God.
Opening doors
wherein we embrace
our family-world.

COME, LOVER DIVINE!

Reflection:

I know my longing for God, but do I realize God's longing for me?
Worthiness is not the issue for God. Love is!

....

....

....

....

....

....

....

....

There are still many other things that Jesus did, yet if they were written about in detail, I doubt there would be enough room in the entire world to hold the books to record them (Jn 21:25).

PRAYER TO THE HOLY SPIRIT

Spirit of God—
eternal flame of zeal
that leads us
day and night
on desert journeys
to the kingdom
promised land;
that burns the mark
of holiness
into new flesh
brightening our hopes
with eternal light.

COME, FIRE OF GOD!

Reflection:

I am the place where dreams become reality and ideals have possibility.

Holiness is the freedom to be ordinary.

....

....

....

....

....

....

....

VIGIL OF PENTECOST

On the last day of the festival, the great day, while Jesus was standing there, he cried out, "Let anyone who is thirsty come to me, and let the one who believes in me drink" (Jn 7:37–38, NRSV).

PRAYER TO THE HOLY SPIRIT

Come, Holy Spirit—

Breathe
your healing.
Drive us
from our narrow ways.
Touch us
in our faint of heart.
Gift us
with divine inspiration.
Love us
to life and
burn
within us . . .
until our dying embers
are held
in the heart of God.
There
you will breathe
new life, once again. Amen!

Reflection:

Each time I experience my nothingness, my creator God says, "Let there be life!"

The Word of God articulates divine love through me.

....

....

PENTECOST

Spirit of God
who bursts into rooms
of fear, laughing life...
your birth-cry
still echoes in
this womb of earth
as we anticipate
the dance of fire.

Sigh in our souls
today, O God.
Throw open the doors.
Slip into our hearts
and sweep grace
into those secret places
known only to you.

We stand on tip-toe
straining, longing to see,
to feel the flame...
praying it will consume
and transform us
into gifts for one another.

Greet us with wisdom
that we may be channels
of peace.
Encourage us with
    understanding
that we may affirm
one another.
Support us with counsel
that we may choose
the good.
Sustain us with fortitude
that we may pursue
what is just.
Open our minds with
    knowledge
that we may realize
you are God.
Bless us with devotion
that we may always
cling to you.
Anoint us with reverence
that we may bow
before the holy within
and around us. Amen.

THE

FEAST

AND

SOLEMNITIES

USUALLY OCCURRING DURING THE

LENTEN–EASTER

SEASON

What's in a Name?

A man called Jesus is named "messiah, son of the living God." A man called Simon is named "Peter—Rock." In this remarkable exchange, Jesus, like the wise man of the parable, chooses to build his house, the church, on Peter the Rock, foreseeing that when the torrents came and the winds blew and buffeted that house, it would not collapse.

We might wonder about that choice when we recall Peter's impetuosity, his rash protests of loyalty, and his craven denial. But we are reassured when we see Peter's tears of remorse and hear his simple affirmation: "Lord, you know everything; you know that I love you" (Jn 21:17).

In that spirit of humble trust, Peter assumed his role as source of strength and source of unity in the infant church. In that same spirit, other men have succeeded him, men with other names: Linus, Boniface, Innocent, Benedict, Leo, Pius, Gregory and John Paul, among others. From the Chair of Peter, these men have shepherded the church through the centuries. Despite heresies and schisms, wars and revolutions, and the fierce impact of historical and cultural changes in the world, the church has grown and endured.

It continues in every age to embody the truth of the gospel message and the Lord's spirit of compassion for all, especially the poor and the powerless. In the person of the pope, Peter continues to stand out as the church's unchanging sign of unity, despite the amazing diversity of its members. We call him Bishop of Rome, our Holy Father, Chief Shepherd, and Servant of the Servants of God. It is to him that the Lord says over and over again: "Feed my lambs, feed my sheep."

GOSPEL: Mt 16:13–19

"You are Peter, the rock on which I will build my church; the gates of hell will not hold out against it" (Mt 16:18).

God of the church,
whose cathedral
is founded on rock
but formed by human life—
through
one such as Peter
you image both
our reality
and our hope.
There
our foundation
is set firm
in life touching faith
and
faith teaching life.

We your church
still walk on water
yet often
sink into doubt.
We enjoy
the grace of change
yet are caught
by stubborn will.
We laugh
the joy of love
yet limit
our fare of forgiveness.

Yet knowing all this,
we continue
to cast nets
into the sea
of brother and sister
to gather
what is broken
and celebrate
what is found.

Have mercy on us,
O God.
Have mercy
on the mystery
that we are
to ourselves,
for it is
in bread broken
and stories shared
that we discover
the wonder of grace
in our hearts.

Guide us
by the wisdom
of your Spirit
who threads us through
the eye of human storms
that your home within us
may never be destroyed.
Amen.

Reflection:

Is it that I am always looking for answers, or that new questions always arise?

....

....

....

How Can This Be?

The carpenter of Nazareth suddenly stands on the threshold of mystery: an angel announces that his intended wife has conceived a child by the power of the Holy Spirit, a child that will save the world from its sin. In the rush of questions that invade his mind and heart, there is only one certainty: his profound trust in the power and goodness of God. He does not ask how or why. He simply entrusts his life to the Lord, and then goes to offer support and comfort to Mary.

In the ensuing months and years, Joseph would have many occasions to wonder why he had been chosen to walk with Mary through the challenging circumstances surrounding the birth of Jesus, the flight to Egypt and the return to Nazareth. Long after angel voices were silent, he would listen in prayer for wisdom and guidance in fulfilling his role as husband and foster-father.

With eyes of faith, he could see God's plan unfolding as Jesus grew to adulthood. He knew how important it was for him to provide a strong and consistent example of faith and trust, as this young man was being fashioned in mind and spirit for the work which he had been sent to accomplish. Joseph never faltered, not because he was enamored of his own abilities, but because he was so confident of God's ever-present providence.

We may often be tempted to ask: "How can this be?" when we are faced with difficult challenges or decisions. We may doubt our own ability or worthiness. We need only think about the strong, quiet presence of Joseph at the very heart of the story of the incarnation to reassure us that with God all things are possible.

GOSPEL: Mt 1:16, 18–21, 24a or Lk 2:41–51a

The angel of the Lord appeared in a dream and said to him: "Joseph, son of David, have no fear about taking Mary as your wife. It is by the Holy Spirit that she has conceived this child" (Mt 1:20).

Father Joseph,
humble bearer
of the trust—
tender love taught
you to embrace
the surprise
of your promised-one,
for you desired
decisions blest
with the grace
of time.
Pray for us!

Father Joseph,
humbled by
the weight of trust—
you offer us
wisdom nurtured
in an evening's rest,
animated by an angel's word
and brought to birth
through the gift
of dreams.
Pray for us!

Father Joseph,
gently open
to the trust—
Mary's words to you
were not
deafened by justice,
but defended
by a dignity
which espoused
spirit and law
in marriage ecstasy.
Pray for us!

Father Joseph,
courageous believer
in the trust—
you lifted Mary
free from tyranny
wrought by wagging heads
and so
confirmed the trust,
embraced the cost
and together
received the mystery.
Pray for us!

Father Joseph—
lover and dreamer,
just man of God . . .
help us to realize
that being human
is not an excuse
to fall short
but rather
a height to be reached
as we are challenged
to walk humbly
with that trust. Amen.

Reflection:
I, too, have been entrusted with God-life . . .

....

Woman Between the Times

Mary stands at the watershed of history. Before her, centuries of promise and hope; after her, the unfolding of fulfillment in the person of her Son, Jesus, the Christ. Before her, searching the horizon for the promised messiah; after her, the glare of the Son of justice scattering the darkness of sin and death.

To this young woman of Nazareth comes the voice of God announcing that the desired of nations will take flesh in her womb and be cradled in her love—if she will say "yes." She will be mother to God-made-man—if she will say "yes." She will fashion the body, heart and mind of the Savior—if she will say "yes."

Mary's response: "Let it be done to me..." reflects much more than passive submission. She embraces Yahweh's invitation with grace-filled eagerness, consecrating the fullness of her being to his service. She seeks no explanations or assurances. She sets off down the road of risk, drawing upon a trust rooted in faith and prayer.

Her journey remains a timeless model of discipleship for all of us. Each step of the way, she walked in the presence of her God, reflected in the words and works of his Son—and hers. Nothing diminished her initial dedication and fervor—no pain, no sorrow, no obstacle, no sacrifice. Her fidelity endured from Bethlehem to Nazareth to Jerusalem to Calvary—and was finally rewarded when she looked into the eyes of the risen Christ.

Angels of annunciation often come to us on our journey. In so many ways, in so many circumstances, God waits upon our "yes" for the particular work of salvation for which we have been chosen. May our response always mirror that of Mary. May we imitate her prayerful trust. May we share her reward!

GOSPEL: Lk 1:26–38

The angel [said] to her: "Do not fear, Mary. You have found favor with God. You shall conceive and bear a son and give him the name Jesus" (Lk 1:30–31).

Mother of God...
mother of mystery
wrapped in angel-wings—
you invite us
to hear the word
of God whispered
in the womb
of our hearts.

You show us
that presence
to the moment
unwraps
the moment's present
and
gifts are exchanged
in the "yes"
of life.

Mother of God...
lady of love
that led you
through darkness
of disbelief—
you offer the
unexpected
as a chalice
of opportunity
to be filled
by the freedom
of possibility.

You remind us
to take time—
to rest
in the mysteries
of human life,
for then
fear falls away
and courage becomes
the hand
that carries us forth.

Mother of God...
keeper of memories
yet teacher
of what we must release—
you share with us
the wisdom
of honoring the past
by weaving it
through the tapestry
of each day,
weeping not over
yesterday
but wedding it
to the hope
of tomorrow.

Mother of God...
pray for us
now and through the hour
of our death. Amen.

Reflection:

Do I realize that the joyful surprises and the difficult mysteries of life are equally wrapped in grace?

....

....

Constance, Anita M.
    Paschal exp.